T0198822

To order additional copies of this book, contact:
Xlibris
844-714-8691
www.Xlibris.com
Orders@Xlibris.com

ISBN: Softcover   978-1-4257-1521-2
         Hardcover   978-1-4257-1520-5

Library of Congress Control Number: 2006904021

Print information available on the last page

Rev. date: 06/29/2023

PRINCE,
A Working cat

by Alice Axenfield-Storm
Photography by the author

PRINCE, A WORKING CAT

This book is about Prince. He is one of the most wonderful and amazing cats in the world.

Twelve years ago Prince was an indoor cat. One day he got out and disappeared for 3 weeks. When he returned home he was dragging his hind legs. Immediately, his owner took him to the animal hospital. After many weeks the veterinarian (animal doctor) made Prince almost as good as new, but nothing could fix his broken back. So he was paralyzed from his waist down.

His owner was an elderly woman who could no longer take care of Prince and his paralysis. Luckily, the veterinarians and the technicians and assistants and receptionists had fallen in love with Prince during his long recovery. So everyone decided to adopt Prince.

The hospital became his new home and world.

Prince did not see himself as any different from other cats. In his head he was exactly like before, except he now wore a diaper instead of using the litter pan. This diaper and the technicians took care of his bathroom needs.

He also wore special pants for his hind legs. These pants were sewn so Prince's tail could come out. There were even sweat and biker styles.

The pants helped turn Prince into one cool, sharp, neat and stylish dude.

When Prince left behind his old world for the new he decided to be part of the action and the team. He gave himself jobs. He did not see himself as paralyzed. He saw himself as "Prince, a Working Cat". He became a teacher, nurse, helper and friend to the many helpless, sick, hurt and frightened animals he saw every day. This new life kept him busy.

Every day Prince was more and more determined to do his jobs well. It wasn't long before his name was placed at the top of the staff list. He became the number one member of the team.

UPSTATE ANIMAL
MEDICAL CENTER

FRANK AKAWI DVM
JOY LUCAS DVM
KATE HEATHERTON DVM

STAFF: PRINCE & FELICIA & GUS
DEBBIE BAILEY, HEAD RECEPTIONIST
SHARON CARNEY, PRACTICE MANAGE
ASHLEY WALTON
KATHY BERNDT, LVT
JOANNE MINK
ANNE MARIE McPARTLIN, HEAD LVT
MARIA DORR-DORYNEK
ANGELA STEVENS
GAIL JONES
ALICIA LaPIERRE

With the passing years Prince has become even more kind, caring, and intelligent with animals and humans. He particularly loves children and often plays with them in between his animal duties.

Prince is crazy about his custom bed which is on the floor behind the front desk. This large, simple, open cardboard box has yummy and comfy blankies piled very high. This blanket arrangement is sometimes changed by Prince according to his mood. On top of everything sit his toys.

He is the official greeter for the office. He walks on his two front legs while sliding on his pants-covered rear legs to every one who enters. He does his famous head rub on a human's shoes, as a kind of hello. He tries to make nervous animals relax. He explains (in kitty talk, of course) that everything is going to be all right. He often goes into the carry boxes as soon as they are opened. A few words with the animals makes them feel better. Most of them are afraid because it can be very scary to be in a strange place.

When there is an emergency in the back room he is always the first to report for duty. He hangs around just in case he might have to comfort, talk or sit with a newcomer.

Many years ago, when Dr. Lucas' dog, "Zu", was very sick, Prince would not leave his side. He stayed with him day and night. For a long time after the dog was gone, Prince looked for the large bed they shared.

Somehow Prince always knows which animals are the sickest. He becomes a dedicated companion, never leaving them. This is the natural nurse in him.

"Zu" Lucas
my best friend,
my constant companion,
my significant other,
I will _always_ love you.

8/1992 - 7/2002

If Prince does not like a difficult patient he may tell them to behave with a sudden cat swat. The staff has tried to explain that he must be gentle and not swat anyone, even a naughty animal. Sometimes he listens, sometimes he does not.

He takes many naps during the day. Naps are very important in Prince's life. They keep him strong and refreshed to continue his work day.

One of his forever friends is Gus, who also lives at the animal hospital. Gus, too, has an illness that keeps him as a permanent member of the staff. Prince remembers to share some quiet time during the day with Gus. Prince always tries to be thoughtful.

GUS's

PLACE

At night Prince used to be locked up in a crate in the back of the hospital. He didn't like that so he learned how to unlock the door. Once free, he had many hours to investigate. Sometimes he managed to slide down the basement stairs but was unable to get back up. In the mornings, he was often found wandering below. He probably thought of himself as a night watchman.

Nowadays he is double-locked in the back when it is dark outside. He probably talks to the overnighters and tries to make them think they are at a pajama party or sleep over.

If you know an animal or person who has been hurt or has a permanent disability, let them know about Prince and how he overcame his injuries. He is never sad. He thinks he is exactly like you and me. He is happy, generous and filled with love.

Prince's birthday is April 21st. If you would like to send him a birthday card or an email, his address is at the back of this book.

I hope you will remember him forever and ever. Make a wish that he keeps on doing his good work for a very long time. We need him.

WHAT YOU SHOULD REMEMBER ABOUT PRINCE

1. Birth date: April 21, 1992

2. Address: Upstate Medical Center, Saratoga Springs, NY

3. Main caregiver: Dr. Joy Lucas

4. Best friends: Gus, Felicia

5. Girlfriend: Felicia

6. Favorite treat: Cat Nip....must have every day, will scream if he does not get any, knows where catnip is kept, and if you forget will open the cabinet himself

7. Favorite blankie: Cat picture throw

8. Favorite toy: Black (almost gray from washing) stuffed dog with red heart

9. Favorite hole pants: All those made by Mrs. Dale Walton, Home Economics teacher at local school

10. Favorite nap spot: Cardboard box bed

This book is dedicated to the remarkable staff at Upstate Animal Center. Many thanks to them and Dr. Joy Lucas for creating a loving and nurturing atmosphere where Prince thrives and will always be a tribute to the value of all life.

Thanks also to Sofia Figliomeni, Emily & Stephen Maynard, Robbie & Morgan. A special thank you to Helen Warren for her professional guidance, time and kindness.

A portion of the proceeds of this book will go to Dr. Lucas' charity, Safe Pet Partnership, where she is a member of the board.

The End

Printed in the United States
by Baker & Taylor Publisher Services

GREYSCALE

BIN TRAVELER FORM

Cut By___Iris Marmol___ Qty_____ Date 10/16/24

Scanned By_____ Qty_____Date_____

Scanned Batch IDs

_____ _____ _____

Notes / Exception

_____

_____

_____

_____